Happy Valentine's Day 1983!
Love, Mom + Dad

W9-CQN-135

Bernard Meltzer's

GUIDANCE
✦ *for* ✦
LIVING

Bernard Meltzer's

GUIDANCE

◆ *for* ◆

LIVING

THE DIAL PRESS
NEW YORK

Published by
The Dial Press
1 Dag Hammarskjold Plaza
New York, New York 10017

Manufactured in the United States of America

First printing

Library of Congress Cataloging in Publication Data

Meltzer, Bernard.
Bernard Meltzer's guidance for living.

I. Title.   PS3563.E4495G8   811'.54   82-5158
        ISBN 0-385-27657-5   AACR2

This volume is dedicated to my lovely wife, Phyllis, who in reality is poetry in sound, action, and her approach to life.

A SHARING

This volume of poetry has been forty years in the making. It seems to me now that I always knew I would publish this book, even when I was a kid. Let me tell you a little about myself, because I think that then you will understand why I've known for all these years that I would write this particular book, and that I would write it to share my joy—and many other things as well—with you.

As many people who hear my broadcasts know, I was born on the Lower East Side of Manhattan. Our address was 47 Attorney Street, in the shadow of the Williamsburg Bridge. I guess today social writers would classify that place as a ghetto; but we who lived there in those days didn't think of it like that. To us it was a vibrant community in a wonderful land called America, and opportunity was on every doorstep, if only you would take hold of it and get to work.

We lived on the fourth floor of a five-story walk-up

apartment building. We had one of the better apartments, up front overlooking the street. It was a one-bedroom apartment, and six of us lived there—Mom and Pop, my two sisters, my brother, and I. If a landlord would dare rent a similar space today, he would probably be hauled off to court and very quickly become the subject of a series of newspaper and television exposés. We had no bathroom in the apartment; the "facilities" consisted of a toilet in the hall just off the stairway. Six families lived on our floor, and each morning everyone would rush to line up and be next—unless you were lucky enough or fast enough to be first.

We had only one sink, and that was in the kitchen. The one sink had only one faucet, because there was no hot water. We would wash up there every morning. Taking a real bath was another matter. That was a once-a-week affair. Every Friday afternoon, just before the start of the Sabbath, Mom would heat the water on the stove. We had a large portable tub that was brought in for the occasion. All four of us children would use the same hot water. Remember, hot water has traditionally been considered a luxury. When I tell my children this after they've spent half an hour in the shower letting the water run and the steam billow, their reply is usually: "But, Dad, those were the *old* days!"

In those "old days," we were being raised in grinding poverty. However, since we didn't have any social activists to tell us that, as kids we never realized it. It is true that sometimes there was not enough to eat and that our clothes were patched up hand-me-downs, but my parents thought our living conditions were practically affluent. They had been raised in the *real* ghettos—the ghettos of Poland and Russia—and living standards in America, even on the Lower East Side, while rough, were luxurious compared to what they had known.

We had two things that made up for a lack of money: a mother's love and a father's caring. My father was a natural community leader, but it was my mother who held the family together. She dedicated her whole life to her family. When I am asked to explain mother's love, I often tell about these early days of my life. To me, stories about my mother show that special love at its highest level.

The Depression was upon us, I remember. Work was almost impossible to get. My father was trying to eke out a living working in the New York garment district, but the pay was low and the work infrequent. We kids didn't really know too much about all that, though, because Mother tried her best to shield us from the facts and the worry.

The staple of our diet was salmon. We almost always had it for lunch. In those days salmon was cheap, and for nine cents you could buy a can and make it stretch to feed four little mouths. Lunch was almost a ritual, and it ran something like this: I, being the most mechanically inclined of us, would open the can. Then Mother would put the salmon on a plate and slice it into four parts. Each of us was given one slice, together with some vegetables and coarse rye or pumpernickel bread. Of course, each portion was not quite enough to feed a growing child, but the coarse bread did fill us up. My mother would watch us eat, hovering over us. But never did she take anything for herself. When we asked her to, she always replied "I am not hungry." It was only when one of us wasn't feeling too well and would leave something that she would take the little scrap and gobble it down. She would smile at us then and say, "I am cleaning up the plate."

It was only as I grew older that I began to realize that Mother would actually have been willing to starve herself to feed her family. As it was, she would often go hungry for us, and she would do that without complaint —with love. Despite our poverty, with that kind of mother's love, I had riches greater than gold.

While a youngster still in grade school I learned three valuable lessons that have remained a part of me and of my life; and they are very much a part of this book. The first was that I was born with a natural and deeply-felt gift for appreciating poetry. The second was that many things that seem like calamities in life can be turned into something wonderful and valuable—if that's what *you* choose to make of them. And the third was that, even as a tough leader of a tough gang in a tough part of town, I had a sentimental streak in me that was hard to control.

I can truthfully say that my love for poetry is in a great measure responsible for my success in life. This may sound like an overstatement, but it isn't. Let me explain.

As a youngster I found I couldn't read as well as the other kids in my class. I know now that I suffered from dyslexia. But those were the days before psychologists and other experts dealt so widely with the problems of handicapped children. The only nonteaching profes-sional with whom we ever came in contact was a part-time school nurse who took care of cuts and scrapes.

The only explanation my teachers knew for my difficulty in reading was that I was "a dunce." My recollections of sitting in a corner of the class wearing a dunce cap as punishment for my inability to read still bring anger to my soul, even these many years later.

In those days reading was taught like this: Everyone in the class would open his book, and the teacher would instruct the student sitting in the first seat of the first row to begin reading the first paragraph aloud. The second paragraph would then be read by the second student in that row. And so the reading would progress around the room, each child reading a paragraph. Now, as my last name began with *M*, and we were always seated in alphabetical order, my seat was always somewhere in the middle of the class. That gave me a needed advantage.

For example, if I sat in the fifteenth seat, I would quickly count down to the fifteenth paragraph and start going over it, trying to memorize it. Thus by the time the teacher called on me I had been over that one, all-important paragraph dozens of times. But even so I still could not read well enough to pass. How well I remember stammering and stuttering, and the harsh criticism of the teacher. But that was only ordinary horror. There were worse times for me, times when, say, the ninth paragraph of our reading assignment for the day was only a few lines, and the teacher would say to the student reading that paragraph: "That was a short paragraph; suppose you read the next one too." In a panic, I would have to abandon all my preparation of the fifteenth paragraph and jump to the sixteenth, reading that one over and over again, trying to memorize it.

And each day, as the reading assignment came closer and closer to me, the terror inside me grew and intensified. And because of that fear, many a time I was simply unable to read my assignment at all.

The teachers had no better explanation for my problem than, "He's just dumb." But I knew something was wrong. The trouble was, there was no one to tell me *what* was wrong. I knew, too, that unless I did something about this, I would soon be kicked out of school. I thank Almighty God for having given me a high degree of motivation, because I licked that problem myself, and in a way that has made a huge difference in my life.

What I did was this: Almost every afternoon I would run to the library, take a book off the shelf, and go up to the third floor attic area, find an empty room, lock the door, and start reading aloud. I would read with loud, exaggerated vocal expression, imagining myself to be a great Shakespearean performer—making gestures that would put a ham actor to shame. The books I chose would invariably be volumes of familiar poetry. I did this for years; and over those years I developed not only a greater ability to read the words on a printed page but a great love for poetry.

And wonder of wonders for me, my homegrown therapy plan worked! How do I know? I just have to look at my school record. In the lower grades I was considered a dunce. In the upper levels of grammar school, I became a normal student. By junior high school, my reading level was above average. By the time I was ready to enter high school, I was able to gain admittance to Stuyvesant High School, which, even today, is considered one of the outstanding public schools in the nation for math and science.

So by the time I was thirteen or fourteen I had learned to turn my problems to strengths, and I had grown to love poetry. By that time I had also become the acknowledged leader of my neighborhood gang in the Williamsburg section of Brooklyn, and I knew that tough kids didn't cry—at least, not where anyone would see. That could have been another problem for me, because at a very early age I had already found that a part of me was uncontrollably sentimental. Again, though, I looked for a way to make what might have been a problem work for me. I remember, for example, that every Saturday afternoon my whole gang would pile into the neighborhood movie house. Those Saturday matinees were for kids; adults entered only at their own risk. There were special, low prices for those Saturday matinees, but even so we developed an almost perfect technique of sneaking in, and after a while the ushers stopped bothering us; they came to view us as one of the normal hazards of doing business, I guess.

Of course, the most desirable seats for these matinees were in the very front row. It didn't matter that it was a very uncomfortable position from which to view the big screen; in terms of prestige, it meant a lot, and my gang laid undisputed claim to those seats. Pity anyone who wasn't from our gang and tried to sit in one of them!

However, Bernard Meltzer was never to be found in

that first row; not even in the orchestra. I had a secret place, and for a secret reason. If the feature movie being shown that day was what the ladies called "a one-handkerchief movie," the tears would start rolling down my cheeks somewhere just after the middle of the movie, and there was nothing I could do to stop them. And if the movie was a three-handkerchief or, worse still, a four-handkerchief feature, then I'd be bawling away almost from the start. Now, I couldn't let my gang see that without losing face. So every Saturday afternoon I hid in a rear row of the second balcony. No one else in my gang was willing to join me, because they were afraid of losing face by giving up those treasured seats. But they all accepted my behavior as one of my idiosyncracies. And so the secret of my sentimental streak was preserved through my growing-up days.

My love of poetry and its influence on my life never left me, any more than my sentimental streak did, even though these were not traits that were admired or even valued by my school friends. I recall my high school days—I was fifteen or sixteen—when we boys had finally discovered girls. As you can imagine, tough boys growing up in a rough section of Brooklyn took a special approach to courtship. A fellow was always supposed to act tough; softness was considered a male taboo, and being rough was the proper way to treat the girls as well as everything and everybody else. Anyone who would stoop to some of the tender scenes that we saw in those two- and three-handkerchief movies was suspected of being what we then called a fairy. (We hadn't at that point learned the word "homosexual.") And since even the hint of such a thing was enough to banish you from male company in Williamsburg, it was understandable that we went out of our way to avoid any such suspicions.

Still, as I've said, by that time I already knew I was a little bit different; and I had learned not only that this needn't be a problem, but how to turn the difference into an asset. Most of the boys in the gang I led dated in groups of couples, and they overpowered the imaginations of their dates with heroic tales of victories over this or that member of some rival gang. But I thought more proper topics for courtship were the moon and the stars and the things that make us what we are—all the things I had read about for all those years in the attic of the local library. So instead of dating with the gang, I preferred being alone with my girl; and sometime during the course of the night I would take out a little book of poetry and read to her. It wasn't any of the modern poetry that was then coming into vogue, but the old sentimental stuff. I did it because I had already discovered that it had a beneficial effect on me—and, even more important, I soon discovered that my dates liked it too. The more handsome members of my gang, the taller ones, the ones with more muscles, complained that they couldn't understand why I had no trouble getting dates with the most desirable girls. All through my teenage years, they never discovered my secret. And for the first time all three of those lessons I mentioned earlier seemed to weave together to my advantage: my love of poetry, my sentimental streak—both of which might have been problems for me—and my determination to turn potential problems into assets.

Of course all during those years of growth I had the guidance of my parents. From my work at Stuyvesant High School it had become apparent that I had a natural ability for writing and expression, and I decided I wanted to be a writer. In my senior year I sat down with my father to talk about my future. I told my father about my writing ambitions, and he told me about the practical problem of a poor boy from Williamsburg having to make a living. He shook his head and, somehow, came up with statistics that showed that only a few hundred writers in the whole nation were making enough money to live decently. I knew he was right; but I knew, too, that poetry and expression and sentiment would always be a part of me, and of my life.

And I was right, just as my father was. Engineering became my profession. As a young junior civil engineer just starting out in the Corps of Engineers, my first assignment was at the Pittsburgh District Office. I was away from home for the first time, and, tough kid or not, I was lonely and a little frightened by my loneliness. In that office with me were other young, beginning engineers from all over the country. I remember that they spent their time reading scientific journals while I spent a good portion of my time reading—you guessed it—poetry! I didn't keep it a secret anymore. My new friends didn't quite understand what I was doing, but since I did manage to keep up with the latest scientific and engineering developments, and more than pulled my share of the work, my little peculiarity was accepted.

As the years went on and many of my friends remained in one area of work and life, I kept reaching out for new possibilities, new fields, new horizons. I went on from engineering to economics, then to finance, to city planning, to banking, to construction, to real estate, to appraising, to education, to lecturing, to hosting a radio talk show. And as I went along I found again and again, as I had in my youth, that poetry and my desire and ability to express myself not only helped to guide me, but helped me to guide others; and I found out, too, that other people loved these things as much as I did.

I can remember, for example, many experiences at the University of Pennsylvania, where I taught for over twenty-six years. I would nearly always lace my lectures with bits of poetry, and with words of wisdom that I tried to hone down to what people nowadays call one-liners. I found that even at this level—a far cry from my grade school and tough gang days—I could more readily explain complicated technical information in simple language by using these devices. It was not just easier for me but more effective and acceptable to my students, for instance, to stop one of them in the middle of a long-winded answer that was incorrect with something like, "Wait a minute, son; you're making the same mistake as the charge of the Light Brigade." In that short, good-natured sentence, I was able to get more across than if I'd gone on for half an hour. And the same proved to be true in more general, nontechnical situations. If I wanted to bring home the point that life is a balance of good and bad, I might find myself using an expression such as, "A rainbow is beautiful, but remember, it takes both sunshine and rain to make a rainbow."

It's been over fifteen years since I first broke into radio, and it was by a fluke that that happened. I was living in Philadelphia, where WCAU, owned by CBS, was the talk station for the town. One of the WCAU personalities got a better offer from another station somewhere and left CAU high and dry, with no notice and no replacement, and with a scheduled show that had to go on the next day. In desperation, as I've always supposed, someone at CAU thought of me and asked me to fill in.

Of course I had no experience in radio, but I agreed to do the show. As I recall, they paid me fifty dollars. I talked about practical things, gave advice on this and that, read the commercials and, as in almost everything I took on by then, I included bits of my own poetry and short little one-liners summing up life's wisdom. When the program was over, I asked the station manager how it had gone. His answer made me feel a little bit as I had when my earliest grade school teachers had called me a dunce. The sum of it all wasn't quite, "Don't darken my door again," but he made it plain that I had no future in radio.

Very quickly, however, the audience for that show let him know different. And so did the sponsors. The phones at WCAU didn't stop ringing. The public and the sponsors wanted more. And so did I. I loved reaching out and trying to help so many people. I loved sharing with more people than ever before my love of poetry, and so many other things that I have learned from life and by the grace of God.

And now, these many years later, I still love doing that. I am both proud and humbled to be able to say that my radio show on WOR in New York City has a larger listening audience than any other radio program at any time anywhere in the country. That audience has become for me what I call "my radio family," and I share with that family as much as I can both of what I have learned *from* life's experience, and what I have learned to love *in* life's experience.

I usually open each show, broadcast seven days a week, with a prayer, asking Almighty God's blessing and guidance. Each hour-long segment after that I begin with—yes, you guessed it again—a poem. Most of all I like to begin with poems of inspiration. And all through every one of my eighteen on-air hours every week, I share with my beloved radio family little bits of wisdom in the form of my one-liners or shorter poems.

It may be astounding to those who believe the widely repeated nonsense that "people don't like poetry," or "people don't like prayers and that gush," but my staff and I get hundreds and hundreds of phone calls and letters asking for a particular poem and for a collection of my poems and sayings. It is not astounding to me. Because, as you now see, I began to learn very early in my life, and continue to learn, how my deep love of poetry, and my deep feelings of sentiment, and my deep experiences of turning into assets what others see as problems—how all of these things are shared by thousands, and even millions, who hear my voice every day, and who know I care.

And now you know why I always knew that I would write this book: Because I want to share my joy, and many other things as well, with you.

Bernard Meltzer's

GUIDANCE

✦ *for* ✦

LIVING

Every day of the week, when the microphone is opened in the studio where I sit and talk to my radio family, I begin with prayer. It's a very good way to start a day or a night. And it's a very good way to start this book.

A PRAYER FOR BLESSING

Bless me, Lord,
so that I may deliver greater wisdom to my speech,
greater charity to my heart,
and greater compassion to my soul.
May I never take for granted
the days You have blessed me with.
Give unto me the strength and will
to repay You by serving my fellow man.
Help me to prove myself worthy,
so that I may be confirmed once more in Thy grace.
And grant to me the gift of life
to serve for another day.
For all these blessings
I thank thee, Lord.
And for all my large family,
all who read this prayer or hear it,
send to each a guardian angel,
and bless them, Lord.

A DAILY PRAYER

Dear Lord, as I start this day, please guide me.
At all times, make me conscious of the responsibility
I bear. And
if I can do some good this day,
if I can serve with good deed and good purpose,
if I can be helpful or something cheerful say,
then, Lord, please show me how.
If I can help to right a wrong,
or if I can help to make someone strong,
if I can bring joy with a smile or a word,
then, my Lord, please show me how.

A ship at anchor in the harbor
is safe, but
that is not what ships were built for.

Faith in many ways is like a wheelbarrow.
You have to put some real push behind it
to make it work.

There would be no planes or motor cars
or homes lit by electric stars,
we still would live in cold, wet caves
if the world were run by those who say,
"It can't be done."

An ambitious person makes a lot more opportunities
than he finds.

Luck is the point at which
preparation meets opportunity.

I remember years ago when on occasion my daddy
would complain that he worked so hard, my mother,
who had a quiet sense of humor, would reply: "I thank
the Lord that I no longer have to go to work. I just get
out of bed in the morning, and there it is—all around
me!"

WHEN PA SAID GRACE

Saying Grace at mealtime, especially on the
Sabbath, is something that was part of my childhood.
It's too bad most of us have lost
the custom. It was such a gracious ritual.
It was good for the soul. It was good for
the family. It was good to thank the Lord
for the bounty on the table. So let me take
you back to days of old. Let me tell you what
it was like when Pa said Grace.

When Pa said Grace and bowed his head,
we knew he meant each word he said.
When Pa said Grace we all could feel
much more enjoyment in our meal;
for he was earnest, and his strong face
shone with thankfulness.

When Pa said Grace, his words were few,
but they would touch you through and through.
He'd simply ask God to bless
family and friends. It was like a caress.
Then, "Bless this food, O Lord," he'd say,
"For all Thy bounty, we thank Thee this day."

Pa has since passed away, and Mother, too.
And now at mealtime I sit at table's head
and marvel at the abundance spread
before me. But before we start
and those eager hands reach out for food,
Ma will look at me and say,
"Children, we will pause a moment now
while Pa says Grace."

Here's one way that's guaranteed to make you value your home more: Go out and price some new ones.

Anyone can build a house.
But to build a home, you need
a loving mother,
a caring father,
and the blessings of the Lord.

HOME

I first saw the light of day
in a fifth floor walk-up tenement
on the Lower East Side of New York.
There were six of us
in that one-bedroom apartment.
But we were not crowded;
and company was always coming to stay with us
for weeks at a time.
And when someone would call attention
to the crowded apartment,
my mother would answer:
"Where there is room in the heart,
there is always room in the house."
After that
the only replies were smiles.

MY GOLDEN RULE

Do all the good you can
By all the means you can
In all the ways you can
In all the places you can
At all times you can
To all the people you can
As long as you can.

When you forgive,
you in no way change the past—
but you sure do change the future.

Many, *many* more people get run down by gossip
than by automobiles.

My grandfather
used to say:
A person should endeavor to live
so that when his time comes to die,
even the undertaker will be sorry
to see him go.

There is no better exercise for your heart
than reaching down
and helping to lift someone up.

Happiness is like a kiss.
You must share it
to enjoy it.

Here's one human characteristic
that almost all of us have:
We are quick to blame others
for our failures,
but we are very slow
to credit others for our success.

I really cannot give you the formula for success.
But I can give you the formula for failure.
It's this:
Try to please everyone.

This I have observed during the many years of my
life:
He who trusts his fellow men
makes far fewer mistakes
than he who distrusts them.

These days you need a sheepskin
to keep the wolf from your door.

The real measure of a person's wealth is
how much he would be worth
if he lost all his money.

As we go through life we find that
the bigger a man's head
the easier it is to fill his shoes.

Good morale is when
your hands and feet keep working
when your head says it can't be done.

Opportunity never knocks for the person
who doesn't give a rap.

The future is not in the job.
The future is in the person who holds the job.

DON'T BE CYNICAL, BUT . . .

When a person tells you that he got rich
through hard work, ask him, "Whose?"

Many people quit looking for work
the day after they find a job.

Here's a capsule of today's economic world:
These days, most people want
less to do,
more time to do it,
and more pay for not getting it done.

Here's a rule that an executive quickly learns
from the school of hard knocks:
When in doubt, mumble.
When in real trouble, delegate.

If life hands you a lemon,
Don't bemoan your fate
Use it and make lemonade.

You will find that, as a rule, those who complain about the way the ball bounces are usually the ones who dropped it.

One of the biggest mistakes you can make in life
Is to believe that you are working for someone else.
No matter what be your job
You are working for yourself.
That's the way you make progress.

REMEMBER THIS:

Today's trying times
in about twenty years
will have become
"The good old days."

THE EDUCATION OF AN ENGINEER

I started my adult life as a civil engineer. So, I said, I must have an explanation for everything. If there was no explanation for a thing, then I would degrade it and say it was mere superstition. I was young, about twenty-four, and I thought I knew everything. It took me twenty-five more years to become a wiser human being—to understand life, the mystery of life. Now I know that there are many things beyond my understanding. So as I start my day I often remind myself that I do not know all the meaning of all these things, or of others that shape my life.

Life sometimes is funny:
You work hard for so many years
toward a certain goal.
And then somebody moves the posts on you.

We are told:
To keep our eye on the ball,
our ear to the ground,
our shoulders to the wheel,
our nose to the grindstone,
our head on the level,
our feet on the ground.
The wonder is:
That we can get any work done
in such a ridiculous position.

THIS IS THE AMERICAN DREAM

You start out by working faithfully eight hours a day
so you will eventually get to be boss
so that you, too, may have the privilege of working
    sixteen hours a day.

Money can't buy
love, health, or happiness.
Nor can it buy what it did last year.

You grow up
the day you have
your first real laugh
—at yourself.

Here is a true way to measure the greatness of this
  beloved land.

Count the number of people trying to get in
Compared to the number trying to get out.
Use that same criterion
  and apply it to other countries
  and give them a score.

A PRAYER FOR OUR PRESIDENT

Dear God

Today America witnessed the inauguration of a new
    president.

I thank Thee for bringing us to this day.

The reins of Government have been turned over
    peacefully.

This is the American way.

This is the way in which Thou hast guided us.

Please grant unto our President the strength to serve
    in the coming four years,

Deliver greater wisdom to his speech and his mind,

Expand the charity of his heart,

Give our President greater compassion to see the
    plight of the less fortunate.

At the same time help us to strengthen our faith in
    each other.

In this land that flows with abundance,

Guided by Thy Grace, oh Lord,

And with the leadership of our new President,

May we all live in peace

And may we all inhabit this wonderful land as
    brothers.

Bless those we have chosen to govern us

Bless those we have elected to lead.

The strength of America is in its justice.

God bless this land,
God bless our President
So that in unison, and with one voice,
Our prayer shall rise to Heaven, to
The one God who has brought us to this blessed day.

Communist Russia has officially abolished God.
But so far, God has been more tolerant to Russia.

The problem of being a leader today is that
you can't be sure
whether the people are following you
or chasing you.

One of the great virtues of our democratic system
is that only one of the candidates gets elected.

At this point it appears that the American taxpayer
will be one of the first
of this country's natural resources
to be completely exhausted.

Worry is like a rocking chair.
It gives you something to do
But doesn't get
    you anywhere.

A true friend is
Someone who thinks that you are a good egg even
  though
He knows that you are slightly cracked.

The reason many people do not recognize
  opportunity when it shows up
Is that usually it appears in the form of hard work.

Remember, there is a big difference
between free speech
and cheap talk.

The grass may be greener
in the other fellow's yard.
But life has a way of balancing up.
He has to cut the grass more often.

For some people,
life insurance is something
that keeps them
poor all their life
so that they can die rich.

Here's a lesson in economics:
A recession is when your neighbor loses his job.
A depression is when you lose your job.
A panic is when your wife loses her job.

And here's another lesson in today's economics:
If you owe $100 you are a piker.
If you owe $100,000 you are a businessman.
If you owe $100,000,000 you are a tycoon.
If you owe $100 billion, then you are the U.S.
Government.

Forbidden fruit is responsible
for getting many a person
into a bad jam.

Following the path of least resistance is what makes
men and rivers crooked.

It is often surprising to find the great heights
that a person can attain by merely being on the
level.

People who try to do something but fail
are infinitely better off
than those who try to do nothing and succeed.

There is no right way to do the wrong thing.

REMEMBER

As we all enter this life
God asks no one
whether he will accept life.
This is not the choice.
The only choice you have
as you go through life is
how will you live it.

There is really only one person in this world who
   can defeat you.
And that is yourself.

The best way to command respect
is to be worthy of it.

You can make more friends in two months by
   becoming
really interested in other people, than you can
   in two years
by trying to get other people interested in
   you.

The road to success is a steady uphill climb.
Unless your father owns the company.

Usually
A conference is a meeting at which people talk
about things they should be doing.

WORK

Hard work is often the easy work you did not do at the proper time.

It is not doing what you like, but liking what you do, that is the secret of happiness.

A PRAYER AT MORNING

Dear Lord,
Guide me as I start this day.
Help me to do justice to the responsibility
That I bear.
Make me understanding of the needs of others.
May I never be unkind to anyone.
May I make lonely folks feel less alone.
And to those who are of happy spirit this moment
May I help make them happier yet.
May I forget that which ought to be forgotten.
And may I be granted the wisdom to guide
    Those who ask for guidance.
May I bring joy this morning.
May I help make this a happy morning.
May I bring peace on this peaceful morning.

The most non-negotiable demand you will ever hear
is a baby calling for his 3 A.M. feeding.

When you get to the end of your rope
tie a knot in it—
and hang on.

Children are small people who are not permitted to
act as their parents did at that age.

A FATHER'S PRAYER

Last night at bedtime
My little boy confessed to me some childish wrong
And I forgave him—kissed him—and sent him off to
  bed.
As he lay down I heard him pray:
"Dear God," he whispered, "make me a man like
  my daddy, wise and strong."
And then in peace he fell asleep.
I knelt beside my sleeping son
Shedding tears of happiness.
As I gazed on his sleeping form I, too, prayed.
"Dear God," I whispered, "make me pure
Like my child lying here.
Instill in me innocence and unselfish love like
  that of a child.
Make of me a better person
So that I may help make this world a better one
For my child—and for all—in this blessed land."
Amen.

The most important thing
that a father can do for his children
is to love their mother.
And conversely,
the most important thing
that a mother can do for her children
is to love their father.

Any man who thinks he is married to a woman
who lets him believe that he is smarter than she is
is really married to a smart woman.

It's pretty hard to keep up with your neighbors
and the bill collectors at the same time.

We may give without loving,
but we cannot love without giving.

The best time to tell your wife that you love her
is before someone else does.

When all that holds you is the horizon,
and you choose to stay,
then you are really free.

TAKE THE TIME

Take the time to think:
  It's the source of all power.
Take time to play:
  It's the secret of perpetual youth.
Take time to read:
  It's the fountain of wisdom.
Take time to pray:
  It's the greatest power on earth.
Take time for charity:
  It's the key to heaven.
Take time to laugh:
  It's the music of the soul.
Take time to be friendly:
  It's the road to happiness.
Take time to love—and to be loved:
  For this, more than anything else,
  Makes life worthwhile.

Many a man accuses his wife of not having
a sense of humor.
There is a reason for this, because
the Good Lord *has* made many women
without a sense of humor
so that they can love their men—instead of
laughing at them.

The best way for a husband to clinch an argument
is to take her in his arms.

One day as I sat musing
Alone and melancholy and without a friend
There came a voice from out of the gloom
Saying, "Cheer up, things might be worse."
So I cheered up.
And sure enough—things did get worse.

Exhilaration is that feeling you get just after a great idea hits you, and before you realize what's wrong with it.

When you think of it,
success is really
picking yourself up one more time
than you fall down.

He who is constantly running after good fortune
and will see nothing else
is really running away from life.

For living is a balance between good and bad.
The wisdom of life is knowing how to identify each,
and which to choose.

There is a real difference between the pessimist and the optimist.

The pessimist looks at opportunity and sees it in
  all its difficulties.
The optimist looks at the same difficulty and
  sees it as opportunity.

There is one redeeming thing about a mistake. It proves that somebody stopped talking long enough at least to do something.

WORRY NEVER

Worry never climbed a hill
Worry never paid a bill
Worry never dried a tear
Worry never calmed a fear
Worry never cooked a meal
Worry never fixed a broken wheel
And worry has never got anyone a job.
In fact
Worry has never done anything that needed to be
    done.
So why do you waste time and energy in worry?

Let me remind you that there is a big difference between being successful and being happy.

Success is getting and achieving what you want. Happiness is wanting and being content with what you get.

Some folks don't realize
when they loudly proclaim
that they are getting
no answer to their prayers
that the Good Lord
has sent them the answer—
and the answer is "No."

IF EVER YOU ARE GOING TO LOVE ME

If ever you are going to love me
Love me now.
Love me while I still can feel the tender affection of
  your heart.

Love me now.
Don't wait till I'm gone
When you will express your love
By chiseling it on a marble slab or on cold stone.

Tell me now of your tender words of love and
  affection.
Don't wait till I am in my grave
For then there will be walls of earth between us
And I will be unable to see or read of your tender
  words of passion.

Then I will have no need for your caresses
When the green grass my face has covered.

Then I won't crave your love or kisses
When I am in my last resting place
But I need them now.

So, my dearest,
If you love me
Love me now,
Tell me now,
While I still can hear
And treasure your tender words of love and
    affection.

For those who are constantly searching for ways to
  be different:
Remember that all it takes is a little charm—and
  caring for people—and all of a sudden you are
different from the crowd.

There is one person
to whom you can continually compare yourself,
and profit
greatly from the comparison:
Compare yourself today
to the person you were yesterday.

Don't worry
because someone starts to imitate you.
As long as they follow in your tracks
they cannot pass you.

Good will
is your own and only asset
that your competition cannot
undersell or destroy.

When you are in the public eye you must expect
   constant criticism.
That's why, when I run across someone who starts a
   long tirade,
I listen . . .
But I often say to myself,
I wish I knew as much about my job
as my critics seem to!

A good way to stop people from jumping down your
   throat
is to keep your mouth closed.

A TALE OF "I DON'T WANT TO GET INVOLVED"

Many stories teach us that often you cannot remain
  neutral;
you must take a position;
you must stand and fight
or you will lose.
This is such a tale.
It occurred in the Civil War.

The army of the North and the Confederate forces
were moving toward each other. A man living in the
area decided to play it safe. He wanted nothing
to do with the nasty war. He swore to remain
neutral. So he dressed himself in Confederate
trousers and a Union jacket. When they found
him the next day, he had a Confederate bullet
in his chest, and a Union bullet in his seat.

There is really nothing wrong
with being a self-made person—
provided you don't consider the job finished too
soon.

Even suffering has two sides.
When viewed from the usual side,
suffering is misfortune.
But when viewed from the less common side,
suffering is a discipline
that sharpens
both the mind and the soul—
and often does lots of good things for individuals.

THE BEST CURE FOR FEAR

The best cure for shaking knees
Is to kneel on them
And ask the Lord thy God for guidance.

Dear Friend who is now far away—and gone from
  me probably forever,

If I had known what trouble you were bearing,
what grief was behind the silence of your face,
I would have been more gentle,
I would have been more caring.
I would have tried to give you gladness.
I would have tried to ease your burden—If only I
  had known.

If I had known the despair within you,
I would have offered you my hand
and made your stay much more pleasant—If only I
  had known.

If I can aid someone who is in distress,
if I can make someone's heavy burden less,
if I can help to dry a tear
and replace it with happiness,
then, dear Lord, show me how.

If I can help to make this world a better place
by helping others their trials to face,
if I can serve my fellow man,
then I know I also serve thee.
So please, my Lord, show me how.

He who understands others is learned.
He who knows himself is wise.
But he who understands others,
And at the same time knows himself,
Is both learned and wise.

When you are observing the action of a good person,
And you see him doing something
you think is naïve,
temper your judgment with this thought:
It is as hard for a good person to suspect evil,
as it is for a wicked person
to suspect good.

Someone once figured out
that we have about thirty-five million
laws and regulations
to enforce the few lines of guidance
contained in the Ten Commandments.

FRIENDSHIP

I can recollect from times past
the many smiles I missed from day to day,
because I stumbled along life's path selfishly.

How many kindly words I lost,
and what joy my indifference cost!

If I had been more kindly to my fellows then,
how many glorious friends
would have been mine years ago!

ANGRY WORDS

Be slow to anger—
Because angry words are like a boomerang:
They return to hurt the one who uttered them.
No matter how hard you try,
You can't remove the poison.
Like the arrow that has left the bow, angry words
   can't be pulled back.
The hurt and pain that angry words inflict
Cling and hurt long after the sound has been lost.

GIFTS

Blessed are those
who give without remembering.
And blessed are those
who take without forgetting.

There was a wise old owl,
and here's how he got so wise.
The more he saw, the less he spoke.
The less he spoke, the more he heard.
And that's the way he became a wise old owl.

For some of us, the greatest underdeveloped
   territory
in the whole world lies under our hat.

My daddy used to say, try hard to be pleasant until
ten o'clock in the morning, and the rest of the day
will take care of itself.

If you have to borrow money,
always try to borrow from a pessimist.
He never expects
to be paid back.

It's true
that to err is human.
But when you find
that the eraser wears out before the pencil,
then you're overdoing it.

The most painful wound of all
is the stab of conscience.

You will find that a loose tongue
often gets you into the tightest places.

When you stretch the truth,
people usually have little trouble
seeing through it.

If you want to be original, just try being yourself,
because God has never made two people exactly
  alike.

Adversity causes some people to break, and it causes
others to break records.

The trouble with being a good sport is that
you have to lose to prove it.

We spend the first two years of our children's
lives teaching them to walk and talk, and the
next twenty years telling them to sit down and
shut up.

Middle age
is when your narrow waist has become broad,
and your broad mind has become narrow

when your children leave you
one by one,
only to return
two by two

when you start knowing you are no longer
part of the jet set,
and have become part of the sit set

when your wife says to you
"Pull in your stomach"
and you already have.

I AM FINE, THANK YOU

When people ask I tell them

There is nothing the matter with me,
I'm as healthy as I can be.
I have arthritis in both of my knees
And when I talk, I talk with a wheeze.
My pulse is weak and my blood is thin,
But I'm awfully well for the shape I'm in.

The moral is this, as this tale unfolds:
For you and me, who are growing old,
It's better to say I'm fine with a grin
Than to let folks know the shape you're in.

How do I know that my youth is spent?
Well, my "get up and go" has got up and went.
But I really don't mind when I think with a grin
Of all the grand places my "get-up" has been.

Old Age is golden I've heard it said,
But I sometimes wonder as I get into bed,
With my ears in the drawer, my teeth in a cup,
My eyes on the table, until I wake up.
Ere sleep comes o'er me, I say to myself,
Is there anything else I should lay on the shelf?

When I was young my slippers were red,
I could kick my heels over my head.
When I grew older my slippers were blue,
But I could still dance the whole night through.
Now when I am old, my slippers are black,
I walk to the store and puff my way back.

I get up each morning and dust off my wits,
Pick up the paper and read the obits.
If my name is still missing
I know I'm not dead,
So I get a good breakfast
—and go back to bed.

Growing old
is really not so bad
when you consider the
alternative.

WHO WILL TAKE GRANDMA—NOW THAT SHE'S OLD?

Who will take Grandma? Who will it be?
I hope all of us will want her—but then I'm not sure.
So let's call a meeting—let's gather the clan.
In such a big family there certainly must be one
But then again I'm not so sure
For you know that old bit of wisdom that says
A mother can take care of ten children,
But ten children find it hard to take care of one
    mother.

'Tis strange how we thought
She would never wear out;
But see how she walks—
It's arthritis no doubt.
Her eyesight is faded
And her memory grows dim.
When people become older they become such a care
So that's why Grandma must have a home
But the question is, where?

Remember the days when she used to be spry?
She would bake her own cookies and make the most
  delicious pie;
She helped us with lessons,
Kissed away our troubles and mended our dreams.
So isn't it dreadful, that she has no place to go.
One little corner is all she will need,
A chair by the window and her Bible to read,
And someone to warm her with love, so she won't
  mind the cold.
Who will take Grandma now that she's old?

What? Nobody wants her?
I hope a nursing home is not her reward, to be
Sent there to await her last days
So she won't be our problem to bother about.
So who will take Grandma—now that she's old?
Remember this if we don't:
Pretty soon the Good Lord will gather her into His
  own loving care.
And then—
Who will dry our tears when Grandma is dead?

The greatest friend
of truth
is time,
and her most constant companion
is humility.

My old grandma used to say,
Time is a great healer when it
comes to broken hearts—
but, certainly, it is no beauty operator.

The good Lord has given me the gift of four score
and two years.
My eyes, my hands, my ears, my feet—are not so
steady anymore. So,
Blessed are they who understand my faltering step
and help me across the street.
Blessed are they who know my ears today
strain to catch what they say.
Blessed are they who know my eyes are dim,
And who looked away when I spilled coffee at the
table today.
Blessed are they who stop to chat with me for a
while,
And do not remind me that I have told the same
story twice before.
And I bless those who know the ways to bring back
to me the memories of yesterday.
My special blessings for those who let me know that
they love me, and remind me that I am not alone,
And help me ease the days as I journey home
to the loving shelter that awaits me, by
God's Grace, at the end of life's road.

So to all I say,
Remember:
As you are now,
I used to be.
As I am now,
Someday you will be.

SMILE

A smile is cheer
To you and me
The cost is nothing—it is given free.
It comforts the weary, gladdens the sad,
And consoles those in trouble,
Good or bad.
It's free to all,
A natural gesture of young and old.
It cheers on the faint-hearted
And disarms the bold.
It's the one thing we keep
When we give it away.

The man who deals in smiles
Is the man who draws the crowds.
He does a lot more business
Than the man who peddles frowns.

Remember the good old days
when it cost more to run a car
than to park it?

Inflation
makes your taxes get larger
and the candy bars
smaller.

ECONOMICS

You owe it to yourself
to become a success,
to make money.
And after you reach that point where you are
making money
you owe it
to the income tax collector.

HORSE SENSE

If each one of us
would stop kicking
and start pulling our own honest share,
we would have little time left for kicking.

In these days of high taxes
we have a new definition of a dime.
It is
really a dollar
with all the taxes taken out.

People who have an hour to waste
usually try to
spend it with someone who does not.

(Very often, coping with life is based on attitude.)

I CAN!

If you think you are beaten—then you probably are.
If you think you dare not—then often you don't.
If you would like to win, but think that you can't—
then it's likely you won't.

If you think you will lose,
chances are that you will.
Remember—success begins with determination;
it's all a state of mind.

Life's battles don't always go
to the stronger or the faster or the smarter person,
but often to the person who
says, "I can!"

Just because you are traveling
a well-beaten road
is no proof that it is the right one.

Just going to church or synagogue
does not make you a good
or religious person.
Any more
than just going to school
makes you an educated person.

You really have to stay wide, wide awake
to make your dreams come true.

THE KIND OF MAN I WOULD WANT MY DAUGHTER TO MARRY

The most important single quality that I would want
the man to possess who marries my daughter is
Infinite kindness.

Infinite kindness will sustain a marriage
through all its uncertainties and problems,
through its disappointments and its stress,
through its happy times, and its times of sorrow;
through infinite kindness flows real love for each
    other.

Infinite kindness brings understanding and
    tolerance of each for the other.
Nothing can take the place of infinite kindness;
    neither wealth,
    nor physical beauty,
    nor accomplishment.

Infinite kindness cements a marriage.
It's a trait that lasts forever
    and will make a marriage endure.
And that's the way the Good Lord in His wisdom
    meant marriage to be.

A QUESTION:

Where and how do mothers learn about all the
things they tell their daughters not to do?

It's very easy for parents
to hear themselves talking.
All they have to do
is to listen to their children.

HERE'S A SPECIAL THOUGHT FOR KIDS.

Did it ever occur to you
that a sweater
is a garment
worn by a child
when his mother feels chilly?

There is only one child that's really the prettiest
    child in the world—
but the miracle is that every mother has it.

DON'T WAIT. TELL HIM SO.

There are times when Dad's days are dark and blue.
He has troubles same as you.
Show him that your love is true:
Tell him so.

Don't act as if he were past his prime.
As though to please him were a crime.
If you ever loved him—today's the day:
Tell him so.

He'll return each act of kindness a hundredfold.
Hearts like his were made to bless.
Why wait? Tell him so.

You are his and his alone,
and well you know—he's all your own.
Don't wait to carve your tender art on his stone.
On this day tell him of your love—tell him that you
    care.
Tell him so.

Never let your heart grow cold.
He's the only father you will ever have.
And when he's gone—it's too late then.
On this day
It's all right, go ahead.
Hug and kiss him—cuddle him.
Really—he's worth his weight in gold.
Tell him so.

A sure cure for laziness
is to have a large family.

I have a friend who always refers to his
wife
   as an angel.
Here's how he explains it:

First
   She's always up in the air about
something.
Then
   She's always harping on his faults.
And then
   She's always complaining that she
never has an
      earthly thing to wear.

Children very often
imitate their parents,
despite efforts to teach them good manners.

One of the things that has gone wrong with modern
marriage is that too many girls get married before
they can adequately support a husband.

Money will not buy peace at home.
But sometimes
it helps to negotiate an armistice.

The Talmud says
That when a man truly loves his woman
and when a woman truly loves her man
the very angels desert heaven
and come and sit in that house
singing and dancing for joy.
And the Lord beams down from heaven
happy in the joy of His creation.

REMEMBER:

Today's mighty oak
is merely yesterday's little nut
that managed to hold on to its ground.

The trouble with people
who have broken a bad habit
is they usually have the pieces
framed and mounted
and never let the world forget.

Nothing improves a person's driving
like the sudden discovery that he is driving on an
expired license.

It used to be that
you worried after
you spent your money.

But now we have invented
something called budgeting

That now allows you
to worry
before you spend the money.

If you want to put your
name to a document that will last
a long time,
then try
Signing a mortgage.

You can't get anywhere today,
and tomorrow will be way out of sight,
if you are mired down
in the hates and frustrations
of yesterday.

Remember this:
The turtle
makes progress
only when he sticks out his neck.

So let it be for all of us:
Taking chances is a necessary
ingredient for success.

There's one thing that almost anybody can achieve
without much effort,
and that is failure.

Top cats
often begin
as underdogs.

The things that
count most in life
are usually the things
that cannot
be counted.

Here is a bit of political wisdom from your sentimental philosopher. The enduring tragedy of our times is that first-class men and women have given first-class loyalty to second-class causes—which almost always end up betraying them.

When a person turns green with envy,
You can rest assured
That he is ripe for trouble.

OTHERS

Lord, help me to live from day to day
In such an unselfish way
That when I pray
My prayers shall be for others.

Lord, help me in all the work I do
Ever to be sincere and true,
And know that all I have done for myself
Must needs be done for others, too.

And when my work on earth is done,
And my new work in heaven is begun,
May I forget the glory that I may have,
And then even more
May I have the grace to be thinking
Of others.

REVELATION

Do you live the way you pray?
Few of us do.
That may be why sometimes our prayers are not
  answered.

A good man prayed as he lay down to sleep:
"Oh Lord, bless everyone and let the sick be well
  again."
And off to sleep he went.
The next morn, he awoke and went on his way.
All day long he did not try to lighten even one
  heavy heart,
Nor share a load, nor wipe a tear.
And once again when the day was done
He prayed, "Oh Lord, bless everyone."
With these words he thought
His obligation to man and God was done . . .
But as he prayed, from on high there came a voice
  that thundered clear:

"My son—you have forgotten my injunction!
Mere words are not enough.
The hands that help are holy in my sight.
You must live the ways you pray!"

This revelation our good man did change.
Now each day his good deeds are many,
For he did learn
That even one good deed,
One act of brotherhood or charity,
Finds more favor in the eyes of his Lord
Than a bushel of good intentions
That do not result
In one act of kindness or help
For one of God's creatures.

Use those talents you have.
You will make it.
You will give joy to the world.
Take this tip from nature:
The woods would be a very silent place
if no birds sang except those who sang best.

Confusion occurs
    when you have one woman trying to make
    a left turn from the right side of the street.

Excitement occurs
    when you have two women sharing a secret.

Bedlam
    occurs when you have three women at one
    bargain counter.

Chaos occurs
    when you have four women trying to split up
    one luncheon check.

Give me a good digestion
and also something to digest.
Give me a healthy body, Lord,
and the sense to keep it at its best.
Give me a mind that is not bored,
that does not whimper, whine or sigh,
and don't let me worry too much
about a fussy person called "I."
Give to me a sense of humor, Lord,
but most important,
give to me some happiness
and the ability to pass it on to other folk.
And may I add,
Give to me understanding of other people's
problems;
Give to me compassion for needs of others;
Give to me humility;
Constantly remind me
that good deeds are more important
than good intentions.

You can never be on top
of the world
if you try to carry it
on your shoulders.

I make that mistake
sometimes: I forget that my shoulders are not
broad enough to carry the world.

I have a friend
who has come up with this bit of wisdom:

He says
modern paintings
are much like women:

You can never enjoy them
if you try to understand them.

This is what is called the how of marriage:

The people who are most convinced
that marriage is a failure
are those
who have tried it
most often.

If you have learned
how to disagree
without being disagreeable,
then you have discovered
the secret of getting along—
whether it be
business
family relations
or
life itself.

Things have sure changed.

In order for you to get in
your two cents worth,
it costs twenty cents to mail it.

One of the most important trips a person
ever makes is to meet the other fellow
half way.

A SPECIAL GIFT

My child handed me
an incomprehensible splash of color
on a crumpled sheet of paper
and I tried so very hard
to fathom the mystery spread before me.
"What is it?" I asked.
"A cat? A dog? A hat?"
"Can't you see? Oh, Dad!" he exclaimed
as he turned it upside down.
"It's a fish, and there's its head
and here the tail,"
and he added with a twinkle in his eye,
"Daddy, I made it especially for you!"
I told him it was beautiful.
I told him I loved his big surprise.
And ten million dollars could not buy
the wonderful look in his eye.

So ponder this:
We are all children of many ages.
The three words, "Especially for you,"
such powerful magic hold
that they can turn the smallest and least costly gift
into one of purest gold.

A person who works with his hands is a craftsman.
A person who works with his brain is an intellectual.
A person who works with both,
and adds his heart,
is an artist.

To be born a gentleman or a lady
is an accident of birth.
To die as one
is an achievement of life.

Greater love hath no teenage son
Than he who lets his
father use the car
on Father's Day.

TO MY FATHER

God gave me a father special
A father who will love me to his dying day,
He molded his heart from the golden sunshine,
And fashioned his smile
From the warmth of a summer's eve.

My father's eyes are shining stars.
And when God's handiwork was done,
He called this creature "Father."
And then the Lord followed
with the greatest miracle I've seen:
He gave this father to me.

TO THE NEW OWNERS OF MY HOUSE

Here is the house; it has been cleaned out in
   readiness for you.
The furniture and everything have been moved out.
The house is empty as far as the eye can see.
But, I must warn you, there still lingers there
A large irreplaceable part of me.

I sincerely wish that your occupancy may be as
bright and as happy as mine.
I was twenty and five when I first crossed the
   threshold.
My arms were strong;
My skin had ne'er a wrinkle.
I was radiant and beautiful,
Eyes turned as I passed.

But now I am sixty and five.
My children are long gone to their own abodes.
My mate and companion has been taken to his just
   reward.
I am alone, except for my memories in this house.
So to the new owners, I say
May you live here fruitfully and with joy—

But if on some quiet night
You hear a rustle, as if someone were on the stairs,
Please do not stir;
It will likely be I
Come back to reclaim
One of my precious memories
That I have left behind.

This is a tale of false envy—something that many of us
are guilty of.

THE WORLD IS MINE—WHY DO I
WHINE?

Today upon the bus
I admired a girl with face so full—
She was so fair,
I envied her.

Then she rose to leave,
And as she passed I saw
She bore her weight
On just one leg.

Humiliated, I uttered a prayer:
"Oh, God, forgive me," I said, "I have two good legs.
Why do I whine?
For really the world is mine."

Then I stopped to buy a newspaper.
The man at the stand had such grace and charm,
His pleasant voice was clear as a bell.
I envied him.

Then as I left he said to me,
"It's nice to talk to folks like you
It is my joy—for you know, I cannot see.
I am blind."

Again humiliated, I uttered a prayer:
"Oh, God, forgive me!
I have two good eyes.
Why do I whine?
The world is really mine."

Later, walking down the street,
I saw a boy of ten or so.
He seemed so strong, and was formed so well.
Envious, I muttered to myself,
"Why cannot my child be so?"
But then I noticed that he stood
And only watched the others play.
He seemed not to know what to do.
"Why don't you play like the others, dear?" I softly
    said.
He just looked straight ahead and didn't answer me.
Then I knew.
He had not heard. He was deaf.

Again, more humbly, I uttered a prayer:
"Oh, God, forgive me.
I am blessed indeed!
Why do I whine?
Really, the world is mine!"

So now when I see people who appear
to be more fortunate than I,
No longer am I envious;
For I have learned to count
the blessings that are mine.
And when I do,
I realize that the Lord has been most kind to me.
Now, as my prayers of thanks,
rise to heaven high, they drown out the envy:

"My God, thank You for the blessings many
That You have bestowed on me.
I am blessed.
Your world is mine!"

A PRAYER FOR THOSE WHO ARE ALONE

I live alone, my Lord,
So please stay at my side.
Guide me in my daily needs.
Grant me health to carry on my work from day to
   day.
Let me be kind and unselfish to my neighbors'
   needs.
Spare me from fear, evil, and malicious tongues.

If sickness or an accident should befall me,
Or if I should feel low and in despair,
Then, humbly, I pray, send me a good Samaritan.

I live alone, yet have no fear—
Because I feel the presence of my Lord
Ever near to me.
My staff and my guide
This day and forever more.

The best way to have a good friend is to be one.

On a Sabbath day it is good to keep
this bit of wisdom in mind:

'Tis not possible to be wrong with man
while at the same time being right with your God.

Remember
That today
Is the tomorrow
That you worried
So much about
Yesterday.

Humility
is a most strange thing.

The moment
that you think
you have acquired it

Is just the moment
you have lost it.

A SPECIAL THOUGHT FOR SUNDAY MORNINGS:

God without man
Is still God.

But a man
Without God
Is nothing.

MY EVENING FAITH

As I grow older
my everyday life
becomes more a thing of grandeur.
I come closer to my God.
When I was young,
I had an intellectual concept of God.
I admired the vault of the heavens.
The stars in their eternal wanderings became,
to me, the symbol of God's power.
And the evolving universe became, to me,
God's message.
But now I am older, and wiser, I hope.
My God is closer to me.
God's hand I see
in the innocent laughter of children,
in the unceasing loyalty of my friends,
in intimate conversation late at night,
in the beauty of many-colored flowers,

in the sound of inspired music,
in the heart-felt thanks that are mine
when I do a good deed.
In all these, and in many other wonders,
I now see the hand of God.

And so now, I thank You, my God, for life and for
     this beautiful world.
Thank You, my God, for coming to me, as I went
     out to meet You,
and for comforting me
as the years roll by.
Now, my Lord, You walk at my side.
Now I need not fear;
for now I have You to guide me
to bless me and
to be my Companion as I travel my life's remaining
     road.

The beautiful in life . . .
   Some talk of it in poetry,
   Some grow it from the soil,
   Some build it in a steeple,
   Some show it through their toil.
   Some breathe it into music,
   Some mold it into art,
   Some shape it into breadloaves . . .
   Some hold it in their hearts.

About the only difference
between stumbling blocks
and stepping stones
is the way you use them.

CAREER

There is a big difference
between a career
and just a job:

The difference is
twenty to forty hours per week.

PRAYER

Dear Lord,
Ahead of me this morning lies a long and busy day,
So it may be that I may forget Thee.
If I do,
I pray, my Lord,
Please do not forget me.

The steam that blows the whistle
is used-up energy
that cannot be used to turn the wheels,

The same is true in life.

REMEMBER

To err is human.
To blame it on the other fellow
is politics.

Before you speak
ask yourself if what you are going to say
is true,
is kind,
is necessary,
is helpful.

If the answer is no,
maybe what you are about to say
should be left unsaid.

A person who knows what he is talking about
is not afraid, and can afford to use language
everyone understands.

A proverb is a short sentence
based on very long experience.

THIS DAY—MAY YOU HAVE:

Enough happiness to keep you sweet;
Enough trials to keep you strong;
Enough sorrow to keep you human;
Enough hope to keep you happy;
Enough failure to keep you humble;
Enough success to keep you eager;
Enough friends to give you comfort;
Enough wealth for all your needs;
Enough enthusiasm to always keep looking forward;
Enough faith to banish depression;
And enough determination to make each day better
than yesterday.

There is a mystic bond that makes us all one.
We are all brothers and sisters
because we all have one Father.

BLESSING

May God send you His love and His sunshine
in His warm and gentle way,
and fill each moment of this day
with love and tender care.

WONDERS

As I behold
God's miracles
I become aware
That this world
Will never starve
For wonders
To contemplate.

TO MY WIFE ON OUR TWENTIETH ANNIVERSARY

Do you remember, my dear,
when our romance was new,
we used to talk of so many things;

Of roses and summers and golden rings.
And then there was music and dances and
    books and plays.
Venice in the moonlight was in our future in those
    days.

Now our world is different.
Our subjects are bills and food,
Patty's measles and Johnny's ills,
new shoes for Billy and a dress for Jane,
taxes, insurance, college, and mortgage bills.

Remember, we used to say that the romance
in our lives would not change.

We were wrong.
It has changed—but in a nice way.
Our romance is more solid and enduring.
My love for you, my dear, is much deeper.
You have made of me an unselfish person as
my need for you has grown unbounded.
I know now the meaning of love.
It is more than music and dances and books and
    games.
I can now truly say "I love you."
Our love account grows with each passing day.
It grows with each new experience we share.
I know this is true love—for the gleam in your
    eyes tells me 'tis so,
Thank you, my dear,
Thank you—
For giving me twenty happy years.
And may the Lord grant me the grace that you
stay by my side and grow old with me.

Every moderate habit
that you have
should be practiced
to excess.

'Tis true
you are only one.
And because you are only one,
you cannot do everything.
But you can do something,
and what you should do,
you can do—
and by the grace of God,
you must do.

LET ME GROW LOVELY—AS I GROW OLD

Let me grow lovely
As I grow old,
Just like many other fine things do.
Like wines and laces and ivory and gold.
And who does not admire a stately old tree?
Old houses with a history,
Are so much more interesting
And have so much more dignity.
So why may not I,
As well as all these,
Grow more lovely,
Grow more interesting,
Grow more desirable,
As I grow old.

Must we know what everything means—
The sunrise in the morning,
Moonglow at night,
The song of the bird,
The hush that falls with eve,
Or the beat of your heart with first love?
The loss you feel when the Lord gathers a dear one
    in,
Or the beginning of life as the seed thrusts up
    through the black earth,
Or the cry of the newborn babe?
Or is it enough for me to say,
Something beautiful passed my way?
It may all be beyond my understanding,
But of this I am sure:
The Lord watches over me
And guides my way,
And I do not have to know
The explanation of it all.
With my God to guide me, I know
I need not fear a thing
Even if I do not know its meaning.

Let me tell you a Christmas story that happened to me when I was seven.

I was living on the Lower East Side on Broome
   Street.
It was a small walk-up apartment—on the fifth floor.
My parents, my two sisters and brother and I all
   lived in a one-bedroom apartment.
We were thankful—for the blessings of America.
   We didn't feel poor.
   We didn't feel deprived, because no one was there
     to tell us how bad off we were.
At school my friends were of all races and creeds.
It was Christmas Eve.
My gentile friends had told me of the beautiful
   things that Santa Claus brings on that night—
   if only you hang up your stockings.
My parents—of strict Orthodox faith—told me it
   was not true.
But I had no toys, and a young boy of seven has such
   hungry eyes—
So I gave in.
That night, just before midnight, I crept out of my
   bed and hung up my two stockings.

The next morning, just as the sun came out,
  I jumped out of bed.
  My stockings were empty.
  I was disappointed.
But my real disappointment came several hours later
  when I went out to play.
My gentile friends
  had sleds, and trains, new gloves and scarves,
  and candy.
All brought to them by Santa Claus.
But I had nothing.
Santa Claus chose not to fill my stockings
  because I was Jewish.
So a little boy of seven went home and cried
because he could not understand
How Santa loved all children—
  but could not extend that love to a little Jewish
  boy of seven.

The New Year for many is a time for boisterous
celebration.
But really it is also a solemn day,
A time to ask the Lord for His blessing for the
coming year.
This is my New Year's Prayer:

May all your troubles be
  as short-lived as the average New Year's resolution.

TELL MOM THAT YOU LOVE HER

Amid your worries and daily strife,
Amid the toil of your everyday life,
Remember to tell Mom that you love her.
Don't keep it a silent thing:
Tell her so!

Remember that at times—just like you—
She has days that are dark and blue;
She has her troubles, same as you.
Show her that your love is true.
Why don't you tell her so?

Don't act as if she were past her prime,
As though to please her were a crime.
If you love her, today is the day:
Tell her so!

Mom will return for each caress,
A hundredfold of tenderness.
Hearts like hers
were meant to bless.
Why don't you tell her so?

You are of her flesh and blood,
And you are hers alone.
Don't wait to carve it on a stone:
Now is the time to tell Mom
That you love her so!

Never let your heart grow cold.
A more beautiful person than she will never unfold.
She's worth her weight in gold
So why wait?
You love her. Show it!
Tell her so!

Let me tell you a Christmas story.
This one happened to me in 1942.
World War II was on.
I was a young Lieutenant of Engineers stationed at
  Cape Charles, the tip of the eastern shore of
  Virginia—opposite Norfolk.
It was Christmas Eve.
The night was raw—cold and wet.
I had volunteered to accept officer of the day duty
  so that my gentile friend could have the time off.
As I rode around in my jeep on that raw dark night,
  the dampness went through me,
But suddenly I was in front of a large tent.
The flap opened up.
The light and the warmth poured out.
As if by a magnet, I was drawn in.
Christmas Eve services had just started.
I walked in
I sat down
I partook of the service
  I prayed for peace
  I prayed for justice
  I prayed that the Good Lord be merciful to me
  in the battles ahead
I walked out refreshed.

The next morning the Jewish chaplain met me.

"Lieutenant," he said, "I understand you attended
   Christmas Eve service last night."

I admitted I had.

Now he was stern.

"Suppose your parents knew that you attended
   Christmas services. How would they feel?" he
   asked.

For answer I replied,
   "Sir, do you think that the Lord God of all
   would be angry with me because I prayed
   for peace?
   I prayed for justice,
   And I prayed for mercy for my soul."

No answer was forthcoming for several minutes.

Then the chaplain—he was a Colonel—replied.
   "I apologize to you, Lieutenant.
   You speak with the words of God,
   I speak in anger; it is not fitting, forgive me.
   You have taught me a lesson."

And that's what happened to me, on Christmas 1942

REST AWHILE

Are you tired?
Then rest awhile.
Sit for a time in some quiet corner.
Shut out the troubles that have bothered you.
Let your heart grow empty of every unkind thought
—and soon you will find that peace will surround
    you
and joy will fill your soul.

Then, count all the blessings
that the dear Lord has sent your way all this week.
You will soon become aware that they are many.
Your blessings this week are far more numerous than
    ever you thought possible.
And then you will be glad that you paused
    to rest for a while
and to let your heart grow empty of every unkind
    thought.
You will be glad that peace now surrounds you
as this week draws to a close.

THE HAND OF GOD

Every time you see new fallen snow, peaceful and
    white;
Every time you feel the sun shine, warm and bright,
or watch the day turn to night and back to day,
or see winter turn to spring, and then mature into
    summer and back to fall,
or hear a robin gayly sing,
or you stop to smell a fragrant rose,
or see a tree, or feel the rain,
or watch the storm turn suddenly to sun,
you are seeing
The Hand of God.

Really, all this is the good Lord saying,
"All this I give to you."
Really these are the wonders of the Hand of God.

HERE'S A TOAST TO MY RADIO FAMILY:

I raise my glass
and to each I say:

May the Lord give you long life;
May you live fully
All the days of your life
That the Lord thy God
Shall give unto you.